Written and
illustrated by
Stefan Salinas

Commissioned by
Nanette Miller

Portrait of
Honora
"Nano"
Nagle

I Am Nano Nagle

Camelopardalis
SAN FRANCISCO

To all of the Presentation Sisters and Presentation People,
past and present,
who walk in the footsteps of Nano.

- Stefan and Nanette

International Print, July 2023.
Printed on acid-free paper by IngramSpark in Australia/Canada/Germany/USA/UK.

Camelopardalis / Stefan Salinas, 584 Castro St. #103, San Francisco, CA 94114 USA
www.stefansalinas.com

Proofreader: Robert Savigny.
Among the libraries, books and internet searches, a very special thanks to the people behind
Nano Nagle Place's website, which is a treasure trove of information on Nano. https://nanonagleplace.ie
Additional editing: Nanette Miller, associates and sisters at PBVM, San Francisco.

ISBN: 978-0-9986088-7-7
Library of Congress Control Number: 2017900563

Artwork: Color pencil, ink, artist crayon and acrylic on Canson and Fabriano, as well as Lokta (Nepal) and
other handmade papers.
Fonts: Century Schoolbook and Georgia.

I see you are looking at my portrait with curiosity.

As it is stated on the plaque off to the right, I was born Honora "Nano" Nagle, in 1718, in Ballygriffin, Ireland. Yes, I was the foundress of **the Sisters of the Presentation of the Blessed Virgin Mary**. Step closer, friends, and I will share with you the story of my life.

I was the firstborn of seven children, the others being David, Mary, Ann, Joseph, Catherine, and Elizabeth.

My father, Garret, came from the highly respected Nagle family. My mother was Ann Mathew, and her family was also from a prosperous lineage.

Oh! I must have been a handful for this noble couple, for I was so carefree and curious from as early as I can remember.

We were not only wealthy in owning acres and acres of land and a large house filled with fine furnishings. Our parents instilled in us a rich Catholic faith and taught us right from wrong.
My father, and especially my Uncle Joseph, fought for the rights of others.

4

You see,

  as Catholics in Ireland
in the early 1700s, we had very
few rights. Our country was
under the control of people loyal to
the country of England
and Irish members of the
Protestant faith.

Map of Ireland

Before 1641

1688

They wrote what they called
Penal Laws.
These laws restricted
Irish Catholics in many ways.
Our horses could be taken
away from us. We had a hard
time buying land and opening
businesses.
My family had been quietly
trading goods and properties with
friendly Protestants, but most
Catholics were left to survive
with what little they had.

1703

Irish Catholic land ownership

100%   50%   0%

Letterkenny
Coleraine
Londonderry
Balymena
Belfast
Lisburn
Belmullet
Ballina
Sligo
Dundalk
Castlebar
Drogheda
Westport
Mullingar
Clifden
Athlone
Dublin
Galway
Tullamore
Naas
Bray
Portlaoise
Ennis
Carlow
Limerick
Kilkenny
Clonmel
Waterford
Tralee
Wexford
Killarney
Dingle
Cork

Penal Laws forbade us from practicing our faith. Catholic priests could be arrested, even hanged! Protestants were free to pray in churches, but we had to conduct our Masses in secret, hidden under trees, away from towns and villages.

8

We would carry picnic baskets and blankets.
If soldiers ever approached, we could pretend
we were enjoying an outdoor meal.
   Our priest had a chalice that could be
taken apart; that way, if we were
inspected, the police would
only find three random
pieces of silver.

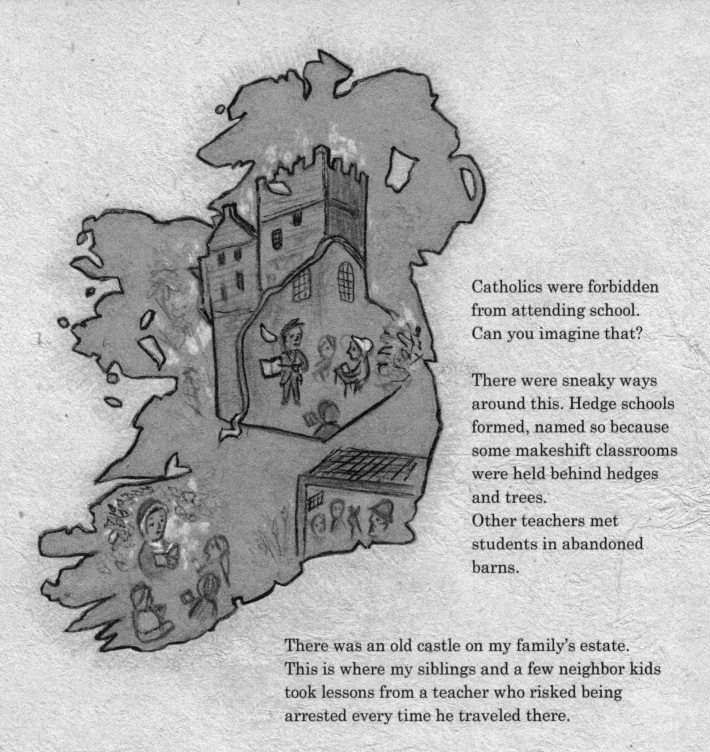

Catholics were forbidden from attending school. Can you imagine that?

There were sneaky ways around this. Hedge schools formed, named so because some makeshift classrooms were held behind hedges and trees.
Other teachers met students in abandoned barns.

There was an old castle on my family's estate. This is where my siblings and a few neighbor kids took lessons from a teacher who risked being arrested every time he traveled there.

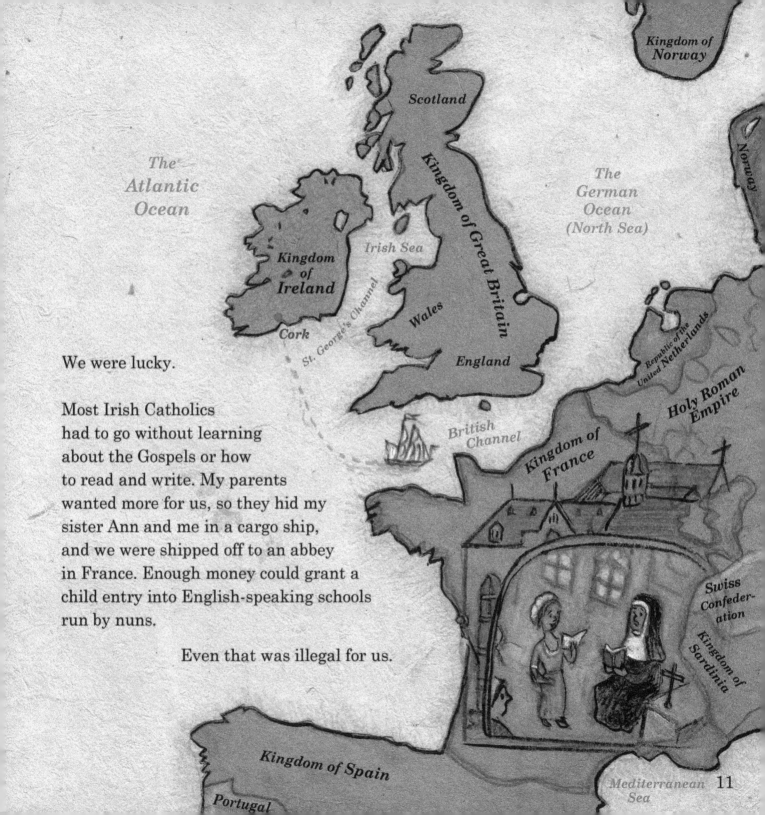

The Atlantic Ocean

Scotland

Kingdom of Norway

Norway

The German Ocean (North Sea)

Kingdom of Great Britain

Irish Sea

Kingdom of Ireland

St. George's Channel

Cork

Wales

England

Republic of the United Netherlands

Holy Roman Empire

British Channel

Kingdom of France

Swiss Confeder-ation

Kingdom of Sardinia

Kingdom of Spain

Portugal

Mediterranean Sea

We were lucky.

Most Irish Catholics had to go without learning about the Gospels or how to read and write. My parents wanted more for us, so they hid my sister Ann and me in a cargo ship, and we were shipped off to an abbey in France. Enough money could grant a child entry into English-speaking schools run by nuns.

Even that was illegal for us.

After our schooling, Ann and I moved in with relatives in the exciting city of Paris. What a lavish lifestyle we lived.

The fashions! The foods!
The entertainment!
Did I mention the fashions?
I so loved being dressed up in fancy gowns
and wigs and attending balls where we
would dine and dance
the night away!

Early one morning,
returning from yet another long,
jubilant night,
a sight shocked me;
it tore open my heart.

14

Huddled outside of a church,
a poor family shivered in the cold,
waiting for the first
   Mass of the day.

This moment in time stayed fresh
   in my memory for years.

Word traveled from home
that our dear father had died,
so Ann and I
returned to Ireland.

Papa gave so much
of his heart to our
family and to the
community.

We cried
and cried.

I had just bought a bolt of the finest silk, and buried my face in its softness, seeking comfort in something that would never give me grief.

I dreamt of the dress I could have made with it – beyond beauty!

The next day, it had vanished from the trunk!

"Nano," my sister admitted, "I saw a poor family in the street, so I sold that silk and bought them food and clothing. I know you will understand."

Understand?? I was livid!

But yes,
Ann was more sensitive to the plight of the poor.
I was so angry!   But I saw the goodness in her actions.

"Yes, Ann, I will accompany you on your walks in the
   dark, dingy streets."
I said this with trepidation,
nervously stepping into the world beyond fine furnishings.
   I left my stylish shoes and gown at home.

19

Oh, sister! Ann fell into illness; then, her soul was taken up by God.

Oh, mother! God took her from us as well! Oh, sorrows within sorrows!

"Lord," I begged, "I promise to do better. I will shed these silly garments of affluence and live my life in service to you. I have been too selfish. Oh, Lord. Oh, sorrow, sorrow!"

A life of prayer,
   I thought,
"I will serve the
Lord with prayer."

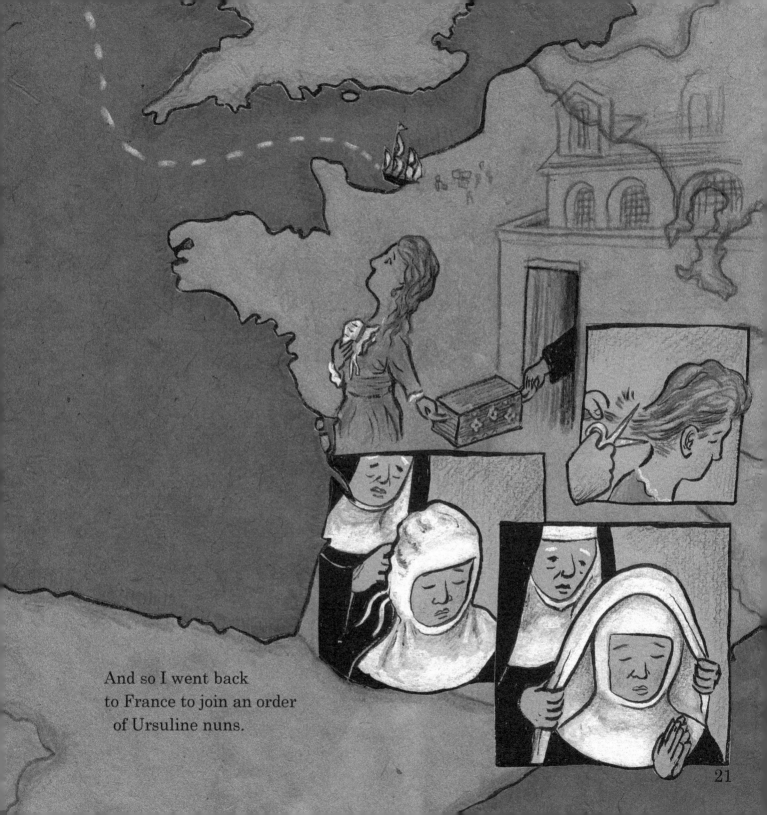

And so I went back
to France to join an order
of Ursuline nuns.

I was a novice, a student of
religious life. Our eyes looked to God
the Father, to Christ, and to the saints.
We turned away from the temptations
of the world, and we prayed for people
near and far.

Jesus,
when you
walked among us,
you were born from
the poorest of the poor.
You shared meals with
people on the margins,
with the oppressed,
with outcasts.

I was safely within the abbey's walls,
but my thoughts kept drifting out
to the plight of the people on the margins,
to the oppressed,
    and to the outcasts.

23

I learned about groups of wealthy women who ventured out into the shanty neighborhoods, feeding the hungry and clothing the naked, as Jesus taught us to do.

A century before in France, a woman of nobility, Françoise Marguérite de Silly, used her money to fund a young priest's efforts to serve the poor.
Father Vincent de Paul, and the widow Louise de Marillac, gathered a group of these wealthy and working-class women. They dedicated their lives to serving the Lord and lived in the community but kept their vows a secret. Thus was born the
Daughters of Charity of Saint Vincent de Paul.

Why were the vows a secret? The Church authority forbade nuns and monks from straying away from their monasteries. Nuns were supposed to be cloistered!

Did Marguérite know that the widow and priest she supported would one day be canonized as saints?

I read letters by Father Nicholas Barré, who opened schools for poor children in France. He gathered women to teach. They were not cloistered; they did not take vows. His schools were built in part with the wealth of a duchess, Marie de Lorraine.

A priest listened to my restless confessions and sensed that God was calling me back to Ireland. I sailed back and moved in with my brother Joseph and his wife.

One day, a man approached Joseph in the street.

"Please help us. I wish to enroll my daughter in your sister's school."

"Can you believe that?" Joseph asked me when he arrived home, "What a silly idea he had."

I said in a quiet voice, "Dear brother, it is indeed true. In a rented mud-floor cabin nearby, I have been instructing - "

He cut me off, "WHAT?!? Are you crazy?

His wife and our wise uncle Joseph came to my defense and calmed him down.

Shhhh.

I present to you,
in 1754,

the first Catholic school
in Ireland for the poor.
Hush now; speak of this only in whispers to people you trust.

26

Like those wealthy women in
17th Century France, how could I use
the resources available to me to better
fulfill the Lord's requests?
I quietly sought out teachers.
Quietly paid for and helped design
 cottages to be constructed.
Quietly repurposed other buildings.

In my life, I was both funding these
schools as well as doing
the footwork!

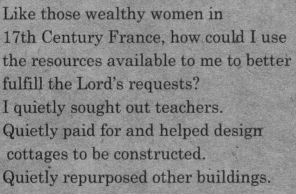

We taught reading, writing, arithmetic, history,

as well as trade skills.

Sewing, embroidery, and lace-making for the girls,

and ship
sail-making
for the boys.

I personally taught
them Catechism,
the foundations
of our faith.

29

River Lee (North Channel)

River Lee (South Channel)

By 1757,
I opened five schools for girls
and two schools for boys,
all secretly nestled
within the busy,
bustling city of Cork.

Some British loyalists and
Protestant leaders
who caught wind of them protested.
"You, Nano, are breaking the law!"

Some Catholics even
joined the opposition, saying,
"Stop this business at once
lest you endanger us all!"

Each school day, I visited and taught at each site.
Oh, Lord, is there ever enough time in a day
to serve the needy?

I would return
home before
sundown,
fix a quick meal,
then don a cloak,
light a lantern, carry a
basket of supplies,

and step out
into the night.

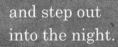

Visiting the
humble homes where
my students lived,

visiting the
homeless, the sick,
and the aged.

Encountering girls and young women desperate for work,
who fell under the control of greedy, older men.
They needed a guiding light out of the darkness.

People began referring to me as
the Lady of the Lantern.

Each of us can
carry the Lord's
light to our
fellow brothers
and sisters.

"The Ursuline Sisters," I pondered, "the order I almost joined in France, they have great teachers. Why not open a convent for them here in Ireland?"

Working with Vicar General Francis Moylan,
and using money left by my late Uncle Joseph, I built a convent for them in 1771.
A handful of nuns sailed to this shore.

Another bold move. The government was barely beginning
to ease its restrictions on us – just barely!

They served children well, they did. They enrolled more and more wealthy Protestant kids. I would never bar any girl or boy from an education, no matter their faith or social status. But they had less and less room for poor *Catholic* youths in their *Catholic* abbey.

I thought, "Here in Ireland, the Ursuline Sisters can continue to pray and teach within their walls.
Why not have an order charged with reaching outside to the young and less fortunate?"

Those secret orders of
women in France,
they would walk
the streets

- not wearing veils
and habits,
but ordinary,
everyday wear.

In 1775, I assembled a group of three women in a private cottage I owned.
Elizabeth Burke, Mary Ann Collins, Mary Fouhy, and I made plans.

Our dress code had to be practical and not call attention in a country still hostile to
nuns. A simple hat, black skirt, and hooded cloak, blend in with the peasants.

We wrote rules for a **new** order, and named ourselves
Sisters of the Charitable Instruction of the Sacred Heart of Jesus

The Nagle family's motto is
Non vox, sed votum, Latin for
"Not words, but deeds."
Our good deeds would be part of our prayer life.

Father Moylan and Bishop John Butler
were quite weary of such a radical enterprise.
They pushed and pushed against it, but I won
their support in the end; thanks be to God!

We four chose confirmation names:
I became *Sister Saint John of God,*
Mary Ann became *Sister Angela,*
Elizabeth became *Sister Augustine,*
Mary became *Sister Joseph.*

*Your most humble
and obedient servant*

Nano Nagle

In 1777, we took our vows.
That same year, our two-story convent
was completed.

To celebrate
its opening,
we invited 50
people from the
streets to a
Christmas day feast.

Oh, Lord,
there are still so
many in need!

My friends and I were only growing older. What about the ailing, aging women, widowed, alone, and without enough food or shelter?

An almshouse was to be built. It must be done!

Running low on money for this, like a beggar, I took to going door to door, asking merchants for donations. This caused a stir in one store.

A clerk was about to throw me to the curb when the shop owner appeared, recognized me, and exclaimed,

"Fool! This is no tramp. This is the honorable and fearless Nano Nagle! Of course, I will assist!"

If only more of us could see the inherent worth in everyone we meet.

As the Holy Spirit would have it, this new house was also fit for my quickly aging self.

All those days and nights walking in the cold got to my breath and poor legs. I hid my coughing from view as best I could. Friends, please, when helping others, do not neglect your own health.

My lungs could take the tuberculosis no longer.

On April 26, 1784, at age 66, I said,
"Love one another as you have hitherto done. Spend yourself for the poor."

My body gave out, and my soul was lifted up to the Lord.

When the order was finally approved by Rome in 1805, its name was changed to

The Sisters of the Presentation of the Blessed Virgin Mary.

The Presentation Sisters use an acorn as a symbol of hope, faith, and hard work. Plant it, and a massive, expanding oak tree will grow.

The one convent, seven schools, and almshouse spread to the creation of numerous convents and schools throughout Ireland.

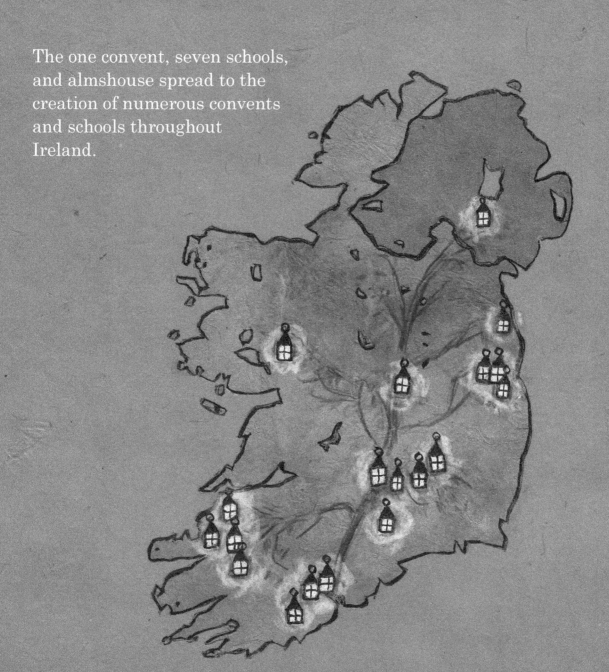

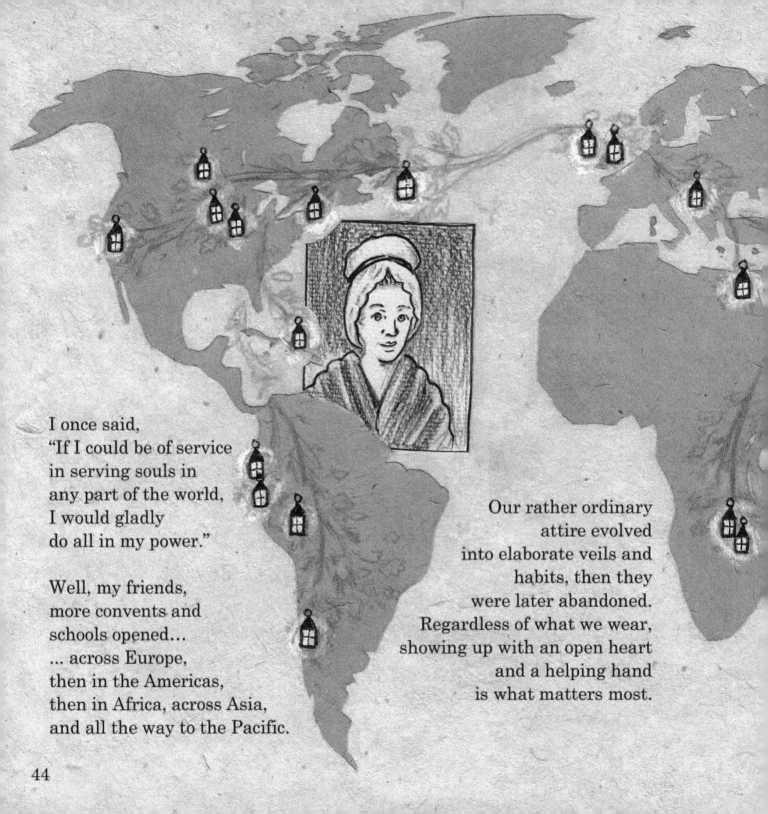

I once said,
"If I could be of service
in serving souls in
any part of the world,
I would gladly
do all in my power."

Well, my friends,
more convents and
schools opened...
... across Europe,
then in the Americas,
then in Africa, across Asia,
and all the way to the Pacific.

Our rather ordinary
attire evolved
into elaborate veils and
habits, then they
were later abandoned.
Regardless of what we wear,
showing up with an open heart
and a helping hand
is what matters most.

A case for my canonization - possible sainthood - opened in 1984. I am currently formally referred to as the *Venerable* Nano Nagle.

You can just call me Nano.

Our ministry has expanded to helping refugees find safer lands, helping women escape modern slavery, caring for the Earth, visiting the imprisoned, championing peace, and spreading the good news of the Gospel of Jesus Christ.

45

We are teachers, principals, chaplains, holistic healers, nurses, counselors, administrators, pastoral associates, and more.

As well as sisters, we have volunteers: associates who help us with our good deeds.

My dear friends, light your lantern and carry it forth.

We can be the
light of the world.

Will you join us?